AF441456

I GHOST YOU

I GHOST YOU

I GHOST YOU

Fading to Find Myself

Hasti Leo

I GHOST YOU

I GHOST YOU

I GHOST YOU

I GHOST YOU

Disclaimer

From the Author - This book reflects my personal opinions, shaped by my unique experiences and journey. The views expressed here are not intended to uphold or dismiss any particular religion, philosophy, or concept.

I have drawn a few references from epic texts and spiritual teachings, but only to the extent of my understanding and the knowledge I have acquired from them. My interpretations are personal and should not be taken as authoritative or comprehensive representations of any religious or philosophical doctrine.

I acknowledge that I have not explored all religious or philosophical texts deeply, and this book is not intended to serve as a comparative or exhaustive study of spiritual beliefs. Instead, it is a humble sharing of my thoughts and insights intended to inspire and resonate with readers on their own unique paths.

I GHOST YOU

I GHOST YOU

Acknowledgments

I am deeply grateful to my family, who have been my unwavering support system through every high and low. To my parents and brother, thank you for instilling in me the values of confidence and boldness that have shaped my character. Your support and encouragement have fueled my journey and inspired me to keep moving forward. And to you, the reader—thank you for taking the time to read my story. May it inspire you to embrace your own journey and live authentically.

I must acknowledge one more source for this second chance at life—a truth I can never speak about enough. First and foremost, I owe a debt of gratitude to my ancestors, the silent warriors whose struggles paved the way for me to be here today. It's easy to see birth as a simple act of nature, but when you delve deeper, you realize the intricate web of choices, sacrifices, and fortitude that span generations, all aligning for the singular purpose of creating the life you now live.

While I firmly believe in destiny and the predestined nature of our birth, I also understand that every single moment is shaped by decisions—both our own and those of the ones who came before us. Imagine if even one of my ancestors had chosen a different path, taken a different turn in their journey, or made a choice that seemed insignificant at the time—the intricate threads of fate would have shifted. I would not be here today, in this very moment, living this very life. It's a humbling and profound thought: how interconnected we are, how every choice, every action, echoes through time, shaping not only our future but the future of those who will come after us.

And finally, I thank God—for grace, I cannot explain, for guiding me through the darkness I couldn't navigate alone, and for stitching together the broken pieces of my story into something worth living. I don't pretend to understand the divine plan, but I trust it. This second chance, this breath, this life—it feels like a quiet miracle, and I'll never stop being grateful.

CONTENTS

Introduction

Writing this book was no less challenging than writing my Doctoral dissertation. Dissertation topics often change during the research process for various reasons. Sometimes, researchers find that there is too much or too little information available, the topic is too broad or too narrow, or they are uncertain about the context. When I started writing this book in 2024, it looked different in my mind. However, as my life changed daily, I had to exchange many of the lessons I had learned for the emotions I experienced.

An opportunity once presented itself, consuming my every thought for a time. I dreamed of it, worked hard for it, and poured everything into making it mine. In the end, however, I never claimed that final trophy. It wasn't due to a lack of drive or ability but rather because I was forced to choose between two paths—one that promised fulfillment and another that seemed to promise love. I believed love was the key to everything, the one thing that could hold me together. Yet, by choosing love, I quietly closed the door to fulfillment, unsure if I would ever have the chance to open it again. Looking back, I realize I paid dearly for that choice. The price was years of my life, pieces of myself given freely to someone who couldn't value me in the way it should have, and paths that led me away from who I was meant to be. Ultimately, it was a sacrifice that left me haunted—a hollow ache I carried with me, wondering if I would ever get a second chance.

And then, just when it seemed too late, life again offered me that opportunity—a path not defined by someone else's vision of love but by my understanding of what I truly needed. Only this time, I saw it for what it was. This time, the choice was clear: I would fight for my chance to start again. Though the choice was simple, the stakes were high—I could take a deep breath and step forward, or I could remain in the shadow of my past decisions, wondering what might have been.

Taking responsibility for my life, I booked a one-way flight without a second thought about whether I would ever return to the land I was leaving. I landed in New York just as the world shut down due to the COVID-19 pandemic. Had I delayed my decision by even a week, I would have ended up in a place where fear governed my every move, and survival felt like surrender. The thought of living each day, constantly watching for signs of emotional or physical harm, was enough to drive me to a breaking point. It was as if I were trapped in a life that could have easily swallowed my dreams, my spirit, and, eventually, my sense of self. I was one choice away from a life shadowed by fear—or worse, from disappearing entirely into the darkness that hovered close.

The journey wasn't easy. I had completely lost control of my life, pouring all my time and energy into what I believed was love. Instead of living up to my potential or purpose, I focused on "fixing" people. I thought that was what good people did. I had confused self-sacrifice with selflessness.

The path to recovery was challenging, filled with regret and questions about what I had lost along the way and whether I could ever feel whole again. Nonetheless, I understood that I could no longer live beneath my potential, pretending to be content while sacrificing my dreams one by one.

This book tells the story of that journey—a second chance, a new beginning, and the courage to live authentically. It is a testament to the moment when, against all odds, I chose to start again.

As I share my story, my intention goes beyond recounting events; I aim to create a space where we can learn together. While my path is unique to me, the lessons I've learned resonate universally. Through these words, I hope to connect with you more deeply.

This book combines my journey with the spiritual insights I've gained along the way. It is not meant to be a guidebook but a shared exploration—a collection of thoughts and reflections. Some parts of what you read may echo your experiences, while others might challenge your perspective or inspire you to think in new ways.

However, here, we have a platform to reflect, share, and deepen our understanding. By exchanging thoughts and experiences, we allow ourselves to grow together, tapping into the collective wisdom that surrounds us

Beginnings

Bangalore in the 1990s was a vibrant blend of tradition and modernity. Known as the "Garden City," it boasted lush greenery and pleasant weather year-round. The city was a hub of technological innovation, earning the nickname "Silicon Valley of India." Its bustling streets were alive with the sights, sounds, and smells of diverse cultures and cuisines. Bangaloreans embraced a laid-back lifestyle and loved good food, music, and community.

This was where my journey began, where life moved at a slower, more deliberate pace.

I realize now that my path is not solely my own—it is a tapestry woven with the sacrifices, dreams, and unwavering love of those who came before me. Every choice, every hardship, and every victory was shaped by a lineage far deeper than I could have ever understood at the time. Now, it's time to share the heart of my story—the family that gave me life, the roots that anchored me through every storm, and the ones who, without knowing it, laid the foundation for the person I am today.

My parents—the unwavering constants in my life—embody a love so deep and steadfast that words often fall short of capturing its essence. They weren't just parents; they were my guides, protectors, and first lessons in resilience. Everything I am today is a testament to their sacrifices, values, and the profound love they poured into raising me and my brother.

While my brother and I were young, the challenges my parents faced were immense—building a safe life for us from scratch—yet they shielded us from the full brunt of their struggles. Their resilience is etched in my memory: my mother tirelessly balancing her responsibilities, and my father, the epitome of silent strength, never faltering under the weight of his duties.

Sometimes, the world seemed to crumble around us, but my parents never let us feel insecure. They ensured we had a childhood filled with warmth, laughter, and learning.

My mother's love came from her unwavering belief in my potential. She has always been my confidant, the one I turned to with both joys and sorrows. Despite the frequent fights, I could never keep secrets from her.

She knew me better than I knew myself and could sense my pain even when I tried to hide it. Her ability to love me unconditionally, even when I made choices she didn't fully agree with, was a testament to her incredible strength and empathy.

My father's support was quieter but equally impactful. Even when I moved abroad to pursue my dreams, he stepped into a role that allowed me to fly freely while anchoring the family at home. My brother and I owe our freedom to dream to his sacrifices. He taught me the value of hard work and the importance of staying grounded, no matter how high I soar.

My parents instilled in me an ethical upbringing that valued kindness, honesty, and empathy. While there were times when these values felt like a burden in a world that often rewarded ruthlessness, I now see their importance.

One of the greatest lessons I've learned from my parents is the power of silence. My father's quiet resilience and my mother's ability to endure hardships without breaking showed me that strength doesn't always roar.

Sometimes, it's the quiet determination to keep going—the silent sacrifices that no one notices but make all the difference.

Reflecting on my journey, I carry their love, sacrifices, and teachings in everything I do. Even now, when life becomes overwhelming, I think of their struggles and draw strength from their example. Their lives are a testament to the power of love and resilience—a legacy I hope to honor in my own way.

The Souls Who Shaped My World

When I was just emerging from my teenage years—filled with the exuberance of new beginnings and the thrill of my first love—life threw me into a whirlwind of uncertainty. My aunt, who had always been a pillar of strength and health, suddenly fell ill for three days. Before I could fully grasp the situation, she was gone. The shock was immense, shaking the very foundations of my world.

I rarely speak about this loss; it's a pain I've carried quietly, never quite managing to emerge from the grief. None of us had expected such an abrupt end.

She was the one person who stood by me unwaveringly, fiercely protecting me even when I felt the entire world was against my family. The love she poured into our lives was boundless, and not a single day goes by that I don't feel her absence.

Years have passed since that fateful day, yet I often find myself haunted by a recurring dream where she appears, reassuring me that she isn't truly gone. While it may sound unsettling to some, I take comfort in knowing that her spirit would never bring harm; she was pure love incarnate.

Every achievement I attain today is tinged with a bittersweet reflection. I think about how proud she would have been and how much joy I could have brought her if she were still here. I often imagine how fulfilled she would feel, seeing me thrive and succeed in ways I couldn't when she was alive. I wish I could share these moments with her, show her the life I've built, and express my gratitude for all she did for me and my brother. Her legacy of love continues to inspire me, reminding me to cherish every moment and strive for the happiness we once shared.

I have never truly shared how profoundly inspiring my grandmother and aunt were to me. My aunt, who raised my brother and me as her own despite not having children herself, always exuded a quiet strength. We were their entire world, and they would have lived for our happiness.

Like many working parents, mine faced days when they had no choice but to leave my brother and me at our grandmother's house. As part of a nuclear family with no generational wealth, my parents built everything from the ground up. During those tough times, their only solace was knowing we were in my grandmother's safe and nurturing hands. She made sure we were always well-fed and never went to bed with any cravings unfulfilled. Because of her, we never slept hungry, and her presence gave us the warmth and security that carried us through those early years.

I remember watching my grandmother cook fresh meals three times a day, never once complaining or giving up, even when times were tough. It wasn't until I moved abroad that I truly understood the depth of her strength. Living alone without a partner is not easy, yet she embraced it with grace and resilience.

Whenever I feel like giving up—whether sitting alone in a restaurant or preparing my meals—I think of her. She spent over 50 years in solitude, cooking for herself and creating a home filled with love. I hold immense respect for that woman who chose to remain steadfast beside her children, even when life dealt her unfair cards.

Her greatest joy was feeding us, nurturing us with the same love she poured into every dish. She didn't just feed our bodies; she nourished our souls. May God bless her, and may her soul rest in peace, knowing that the legacy of love she left behind continues to inspire me every single day.

I Owe Him the World

My brother, whom I owe the world, has been my unwavering support and lifeline. Just a year and a half older than me, he has always had a unique way of navigating life—calm, composed, and guided by an unshakable inner strength. From him, I learned once again the power of silence—how sometimes the most profound emotions and the deepest acts of love don't need to be voiced but simply felt.

When I moved abroad, leaving behind the familiar world of family, friends, and the comforting rhythm of home, the only solace I had was knowing my brother was there to take care of our parents. It wasn't just his physical presence but the weight of responsibility he took on that gave me peace of mind.

My parents making sacrifices for me and forgiving my mistakes was something I could understand—they were my parents, after all. But for my brother, barely out of his youth, to willingly sacrifice his lifestyle, dreams, and freedom so I could chase mine—no words can describe the magnitude of that love.

Being in a long-distance relationship with him as my confidant is painful, with the miles between us often feeling like an ocean too vast to cross. Yet, the bond we share never falters. The distance strengthens the quiet but powerful connection we have. Our love for each other remains steadfast despite being separated by time zones, responsibilities, and life changes.

He carried the weight of two lives—his and mine—so I could fly. It wasn't about grand gestures but the small, daily sacrifices, the countless moments when he chose to put our family above his own needs. I owe him more than I can ever repay, yet I know he expects nothing in return.

It's this silent, profound love that makes him not just my brother but my hero.

Whenever I stumbled, he stood taller for me, and his strength became my anchor. He taught me that love doesn't always come in words and that support doesn't always require noise. It can exist in the quiet moments, in the unspoken sacrifices, and in the unwavering presence of someone who believes in you more than you believe in yourself.

Spiritual Life: A Treasure My Parents Passed Onto Us

My parents have always been my guiding light—not just in the practical aspects of life but also in the realm of spirituality. From a young age, they instilled in my brother and me a deep sense of spirituality that has become a cornerstone of our lives. This spiritual foundation is one of the most treasured gifts they have passed on to us, shaping our perspectives and guiding our actions even in the most challenging times.

Growing up, spirituality was not merely a set of rituals or practices but a way of life. My parents taught us that true spirituality lies in understanding and embracing the deeper meaning of life, recognizing the interconnectedness of all beings, and finding peace and purpose within ourselves. They emphasized that spirituality is about cultivating kindness, compassion, and gratitude—beginning with how we treat ourselves and others.

The spiritual lessons from my parents also taught me the importance of gratitude. They encouraged us to always look for the good in every situation, appreciate our blessings, and express gratitude for the simple joys of life. This practice of gratitude has transformed my outlook on life, helping me stay positive and hopeful despite adversity.

While other children spent their evenings playing games and sports, ours were structured with a disciplined playtime routine, followed by yoga posture practice and meditation. Instead of bedtime stories, our nights were filled with epic tales from *Kishora Bharata* (a simplified version of the *Mahabharata* for children), spiritual teachings, and inspiring accounts of patriotism. These stories, narrated by our mother, planted seeds of wisdom, discipline, and resilience within us from a young age.

While many of us may not have inherited generational wealth, I've come to realize that the greatest gift our parents gave us was something far more valuable—courage. The courage to stand tall in adversity, to rise after every fall, to keep moving when the path is unclear. The courage to fight for what's right, to rebuild from nothing, to trust in life even when it feels unfair.

Most importantly, the courage to let go of fear and step into our own power. Because in the end, it's not what we inherit, but what we become that truly defines us.

Childhood Memories of Temples and Ashramas

My childhood memories are mostly filled with temples and ashramas—sacred places that my parents somehow discovered without the convenience of Google Maps. These spiritual sanctuaries became integral to my upbringing, shaping my values and worldview in ways that continue to resonate with me.

Every day, we visited the Ramakrishna Ashram for bhajans. The rhythmic chants and the serene atmosphere of the ashram provided a sense of peace and connection that grounded me from a young age. The teachings of Ramakrishna Paramahamsa and Swami Vivekananda, often discussed in the ashram, instilled in me the importance of selfless service, devotion, and inner strength.

Our weekly visits to volunteer at the Art of Living Center were another significant aspect of my childhood. My parents believed in the power of *seva*, or selfless service, and they ensured that my brother and I understood the value of contributing to the community. Whether helping to organize events, cleaning the premises, or simply offering our time to support various initiatives, these experiences taught us humility, compassion, and the joy of giving.

Prayers and gratitude were woven into the fabric of our daily lives. My parents taught us to offer prayers not just in temples but also in our own homes. We expressed gratitude for water, food, and the everyday blessings that are often taken for granted. This simple act made us aware of the abundance we had and reminded us to be grateful for every bite. It was a powerful lesson in mindfulness and appreciation that has stayed with me. Journaling also became part of our routine from a very young age.

These early experiences with spirituality were not about rigid dogmas or rituals but about fostering a deep connection with the divine and recognizing the sacredness in everyday life.

Looking back, I realize how fortunate I was to grow up in such an environment. These spiritual practices and values have become the foundation of my life, guiding me through challenges and helping me find meaning and purpose.

The memories of those temple visits, the soulful bhajans, the selfless service at the ashramas, and the daily prayers have left an indelible mark on my heart. My parents' unwavering commitment to our spiritual growth is a treasure that I always carry with me— a beacon of light guiding me on my journey.

Memories of Hampi: A Lesson in Resilience

I was around ten when my parents took my brother and me on a trip to the once-glorious Vijayanagara Empire, now called Hampi. This trip has remained deeply embedded in my subconscious. The place, the stories behind it, and especially Kishkinda—the monkey god temple—imparted profound life lessons. The Tungabhadra River and the magnificent monuments of Hampi hold a special place in my heart and mind. Even twenty years later, I can vividly recall this place without needing to look at pictures. This vivid recollection comes from how my parents planned the trip and explained every monument to us. They ensured that we weren't just seeing but genuinely experiencing and understanding the essence of Hampi.

As we explored the ancient ruins, climbed the boulder-strewn hills, and listened to tales of a bygone era, we found a temporary respite from our everyday struggles. The grandeur of the ancient empire and the stories of its rise and fall mirrored our own lives in a way. It taught us about resilience, the cyclical nature of fortune, and the importance of hope and perseverance.

This experience remains one of my best memories with my parents, even though it was clear they were hiding their pain from us. My parents are the most incredible and optimistic people I've ever known. They understood that life isn't always fair but believed that everything happens for a reason. They knew that for the wheel of life to turn upwards, it must first descend.

Like many parents, mine went to great lengths to shield us from the darker side of life, masking their worries and struggles with love and optimism. Little did they know that my brother and I were observant and perceptive enough to understand the situation and recognize how our parents protected us.

Despite our struggles at the time, my parents decided to take us to Hampi. They knew that experiences and memories were invaluable, and they wanted to instill in us a sense of wonder and curiosity about the world. They wanted us to learn that even in the face of adversity, there is always something beautiful to be found—something worth exploring and cherishing.

Looking back, I realize that this trip to Hampi was not just a family vacation but a pivotal moment in my life. It shaped my understanding of resilience, and the importance of finding beauty and meaning even in difficult times. It taught me how to face life's challenges with grace and optimism—lessons that continue to guide me to this day.

It wasn't just Hampi. Whenever we felt unsettled by life, my parents chose not to worry much but instead took us on vacations.

These trips were typically budget-friendly and often centered around spiritual destinations. These places weren't necessarily religious, but they carried a sense of positive energy and wisdom, offering us valuable experiences.

Lessons Beyond the Classroom

When I started writing this book, it didn't take long to finish because much of it had already been documented in my journals from childhood. Each page of this book is woven from those memories, reflections, and lessons I've recorded over the years. It's more than just a narrative—it's a journey through the fragments of my life that I've captured and now stitched together to form a cohesive story.

Revisiting my schooling experience reminds me of the shy, kind child I was until I entered my undergraduate studies.

School was both a sanctuary and a battleground. Academically, I found solace in the structured rhythm of learning, excelling as I immersed myself in the comforting predictability of textbooks and lessons. Pursuing knowledge gave me a sense of stability and purpose, grounding me during uncertain times.

Socially, however, the experience was far more turbulent. I didn't have many friends—not because I was invisible, but because I never seemed to fit into the molds others had created. My differences were too pronounced, too unique to seamlessly blend into any group.

This isolation, while painful, became a transformative teacher. It taught me the futility of seeking validation from those who thrived on negativity and forced me to confront the necessity of self-acceptance. It was a harsh but invaluable lesson: conformity may offer temporary acceptance, but it erases the essence of who you are. I decided to embrace my individuality—my quirks, my accent, my voice—everything that made me who I am.

As I moved through adolescence and into young adulthood, I began to seek greater independence. The values and lessons instilled in me by my family provided a strong foundation, but I was eager to carve out my own path and explore the world on my own terms.

I chose my friends and how I wanted to spend my time. Instead of partying or gossiping, I focused on hobbies that would be genuinely useful in the near future. While I certainly enjoyed my college days of fun and socializing, the greatest lessons I learned early in my adolescence helped me stay focused on my interests and purpose.

In college, I found my voice in both speech and spirit. I learned to speak up for my beliefs, assert my identity, and stand tall in my truth. Every small victory was a testament to my growth, fueling my drive to push forward, no matter the challenges.

Immigrant Life in New York City

The city brought its mix of good and bad. The multicultural exposure, abundant opportunities, and platforms to voice ideas were undeniably enriching. Yet, these came with their challenges: homesickness, fear of subway shootings, fear of being mocked, weakened immunity, and an overwhelming sense of loneliness. Here, everyone seemed sweet on the surface, but no one truly felt like *yours*. Thriving in this city meant learning the delicate balance of building friendships without getting too attached—a skill that, though difficult, became essential for survival.

In this whirlwind of adjustments, my connection to home became my anchor. Everything I cooked started tasting great, and my mom became WhatsApp's biggest fan, calling it a *"five-star invention"* every time we spoke. Technology has become our lifeline. Calls weren't just conversations; they were a presence— my phone would stay live for hours while I cooked, brushed, worked, or walked, just to feel the essence of home.

But some things, like falling sick, I had to hide. I knew all it would do was make them worry, helpless from so far away. It was easier to mask my stress and pain than to explain it and hear the sadness in their voices.

For years, I survived without meeting my family. For someone like me—nursing a broken heart and trying to stay strong in a competitive and unfamiliar world—my strength came through those video calls.

Every immigrant will relate to this: the bittersweet comfort of hearing home through a screen, holding you together while everything around you feels like it's falling apart.

Living away from a loving family presents many challenges, and I found it particularly difficult to adjust to the weather here. Coming from a city like Bangalore, known for its pleasant climate, I struggled with the harsh winters, where temperatures sometimes dropped below freezing. The low humidity made it even harder to cope, as running heaters to combat the cold led to even drier air and a bleeding nose, affecting my skin, hair, and overall health.

Having to get enough sunlight for survival but unable to step out without freezing, I found myself caught in a dilemma—craving the warmth of the sun while dreading the biting cold that made every step outside unbearable. The struggle wasn't just physical; it weighed on my mind, making me long for the familiar comfort of home.

Immigrant life is no joke. Although I am more of an introvert who can thrive with limited social interaction, I realize the importance of networking. Connections can be vital for career opportunities, house hunting, Serendipity, and Emotional Resilience. I had to learn the delicate skill of building genuine relationships while also maintaining a sense of self-protection.

During a tough period—when I was dealing with heartbreak and had little desire to cook or smile for months—places like temples, gurudwaras, and libraries became my safe-havens. They welcomed me whenever I felt lonely, providing me with nourishing meals and peace for my soul. Volunteering, or *seva*, at the gurudwara became a significant part of my daily life. Taking the time to volunteer at NGOs gave me a profound sense of satisfaction.

This city has everything to help you grow as a person—or to lead you astray if that's what you choose. It all comes down to the choices we make. Although the city may not be the safest—given the subway incidents, scams, and other concerns—I found support from my apartment mates, managers at work, and my college support group, which helped ease my fears. New York doesn't promise safety, but it does promise resilience. It's a city that'll test you and then wrap you in its wildly diverse embrace when you least expect it. Here, 'home' isn't just a zip code—it's the people who make the chaos beautiful.

My Love

As a child, I often felt like I was watching my parents live through a never-ending series of battles—each year brought a new problem, like episodes of a gripping show that never seemed to have a happy ending. They tried to shield me and my brother from their struggles, but we weren't oblivious. We saw it all—the worry in their eyes, the stress that weighed on their shoulders. But through it all, we were a family. My parents fought through challenges together while always celebrating our milestones. In a way, I grew up witnessing a successful love marriage.

As a girl raised on romantic Bollywood movies, the love story unfolding in my home shaped my understanding of love, marriage, and family life, creating a fantasy about these concepts in my mind.

Growing up in a nuclear family, my world was small but deeply connected. My parents and brother were everything to me. Being the pampered kid, I never had to step outside the comfort of their love, and because of this, a quiet fear followed me—*what would life be without them?*

As I got older, I began to unknowingly search for that same sense of security in my relationships, expecting my partner to not only love my family but to parent me in the way they did. But in doing so, I was letting my present slip away while looking for someone for my future. I wasn't truly living in the love and warmth that my family was still offering.

It took me a long time to realize that I was searching for something outside myself when everything I needed was already within reach—in those very moments with them.

And then, he entered my life—someone unlike anyone I had seen in my parents.

He was manly in a way I hadn't known, with a strength and presence that drew me in. In him, I felt a sense of security I had longed for, making me believe I had finally found my safe space. For the first time, I thought I had found someone who could fill the role I had unknowingly been searching for—someone who could protect and hold me in a way I'd never experienced before. Someone I thought I could be vulnerable with, someone with whom I could finally let my guard down.

But in no time, I realized this boy needed me more than I needed him. From being the pampered child, I transitioned into a role I had never anticipated—that of a mother. I found myself trying to save him from drowning in his own struggles, taking on responsibilities that were not mine to bear. I became the caregiver, offering support and stability in a relationship where I was desperately trying to fill the void left by his insecurities and fears. Instead of seeking protection, I was now trying to be the lifeline for someone who was meant to be my anchor.

However, I embraced the role—because I was in love. I was innocently, unconditionally, and insanely in love, the kind that knew no boundaries and no hesitation.

I wouldn't think twice if it meant sacrificing everything to save him, even my own life. Every dream I ever had was woven with his presence, every decision shaped by his existence. My love wasn't just a feeling; it was my very being. After all, that was the only thing I knew—from a very young age until I grew into my late 20s. Love, for me, was devotion, sacrifice, and an unshakable belief that relationships were meant to be held onto, no matter the cost. It was my guiding force, my reason for enduring, for forgiving, for fighting against all odds. I had built my entire world around it, believing that if I just loved enough, everything else would fall into place. But life had its own lessons to teach—ones that would challenge everything I had ever believed about love, strength, and self-worth.

Though I wouldn't think twice about giving my life for it, it killed me every day for nothing—a love that wasn't just pulling me away from my dreams but threatening my very existence. It became clear that I was fading into the background of my own story. There were more tears than laughter. As I endured abuse and blackmail, I realized I had lost control over my life.

I still remember those nights, screaming into my pillow until my voice was gone, tears soaking the fabric as I wrestled with the same question over and over: *Should I give up or give even more?* The weight of it all felt endless, the uncertainty brutal. I was fighting for clarity in the dark, hoping for some sign, some whisper of direction. But all I had was my own silent battle, night after night, alone with the fear that no matter what I chose, I'd still end up empty.

For years, I put my own needs and dreams on hold, living like an old soul—worn before its time—battling for a love that I thought was worth every sacrifice.

A Love That Inspired Me

When I was around 14, I stumbled upon an old box tucked away in our storage room. Like many other loving mothers, mine had preserved small tokens of our relationship—greetings, handmade cards, and shared memories. But as I dug through the contents, I found something unexpected: a 28-page love letter my father had written to my mother in the 1960s.

I can still vividly recall that moment. That letter was more than just a relic of their love—it was a window into my own romantic spirit. I now understand my deep appreciation for love, and its expression comes from my father. His words, though written decades before, shaped a part of who I became.

Discovering My Voice

Fast forward to my second year of undergrad—I signed up for a few intercollegiate competitions, as usual. On one particular day, with three hours of free time between two events, I wandered the corridors of the sprawling campus. My eyes caught a glimpse of a large, covered painting in one of the classrooms. Intrigued, I soon discovered it was part of a competition called *Drishya*

Kavya, where participants were given just 20 minutes to write a poem inspired by a painting.

The spontaneity of it piqued my interest. Although the maximum number of participants had already been reached, the registrar allowed me to enter as a last-minute addition.

The judge uncovered the painting, revealing a woman sitting alone.

For the first minute or two, I was lost in thought, unsure how to begin. But as I looked deeper, I realized—this wasn't just a woman sitting. She was a woman in sorrow. The emotions came flooding in, and the first line wrote itself:

"Marada melini jodi hakki naavibbaru, doorada bhavane hattirave iddaru."

Loosely translated, it meant: *"We are two birds perched on the tree, yet though we are near, we feel distant."*

I kept writing, pouring out emotions until the timer buzzed. When I handed in my eight-paragraph poem, I didn't think much of it.

A couple of hours later, when they announced the winners, I was surprised to hear my name. I had won second place out of 48 participants, but this victory felt different.

Although I had participated in and won three other competitions that day, this particular win resonated with me on a profound level. It was as if I had uncovered a part of myself I hadn't fully realized existed—the artist within me.

But that moment also brought another realization. The poem I wrote was not just about the woman in the painting—it was about me. It was a heartbroken, melancholy piece, and I couldn't help but wonder why, at such a young age, I could write about such deep sorrow. How could I feel this pain, this longing, when I was supposed to be experiencing the thrills of young love? Was my love even reciprocated? I was romantic, perhaps too romantic for my own good, but was I truly happy? The answers remained elusive then, but that day revealed more about myself than I had anticipated.

Yet, there I was, still consumed by unconditional love and a mad savior complex.

I wouldn't blame my partner completely for that because, in truth, it must have been me who overfilled the space. I gave so much—perhaps too much—of myself, expecting that love would fill the gaps where my dreams and needs had been pushed aside. I poured myself into the relationship without realizing how much I was sacrificing. In my efforts to give everything to him, I neglected the parts of me that needed nurturing. I stopped being kind to myself and even to my family.

All my focus was on supporting my partner and trying to heal him. I wanted to be the one to fix it all.

But what I failed to realize was that, in my desperation to heal him, I was neglecting my own wounds—wounds I was creating by ignoring my needs and burying my own pain. While I was busy trying to rescue him from his past, I was drowning on my own, unable to see how much I was losing in the process. I thought that if I loved him enough if I supported him enough, everything would eventually fall into place. But in doing so, I ignored the very healing I needed. Instead of tending to my own wounds, I became consumed by his, and in doing so, I lost sight of who I truly was.

Despite recognizing the imbalance, I continued to pour myself into something that wasn't reciprocated in the way it should have been. For a few more years, I clung to hope—hope that things would change, that the love I was giving would eventually be valued. Sometimes, people are so convinced they're doing everything right that they don't see the harm in their actions—or their inaction. In that same vein, I not only let my guard down but failed to establish boundaries—boundaries that could have shielded me from hurt or helped me know when to walk away.

And then, I realized that people can only give what they're capable of giving. I had been so consumed by empathy, seeing potential in what *could have been* rather than acknowledging the reality for what it *was.* I believed in the possibility of change, in the idea that if I loved harder, understood deeper, or gave more, things would eventually align. But the *potential* is just that—an idea, a distant dream. It's not the reality we live in.

Potential is a beautiful thing, but it's not enough when it remains just that—unrealized.

As time passed, the cracks deepened, and what once felt like a fragile bond finally began to crumble. The weight of unreciprocated efforts and unspoken truths became too heavy to ignore. The foundations I had built on hope and potential started to shake, and eventually, the illusion I clung to fell apart. What I once thought was just a rough patch revealed itself to be the slow erosion of something that was never as strong as I believed.

Each moment of silence, each ignored feeling, chipped away at what was left of the connection, and I realized that love, when not nurtured equally, can turn into something painful. The bond I had so fiercely held onto was no longer sustaining me; it was suffocating me. The cracks were no longer repairable, and I had to accept that some things were meant to break.

It's all about timing—if my love had been reciprocated when it still felt alive, the story might have turned out entirely different. But sometimes life doesn't work that way, and you come to realize that missed moments shape you the most. My friends and family always saw how I could pour myself into love, how every word I spoke or wrote carried the weight of emotions left unspoken.

I was the dreamer—the one who believed in grand gestures, in the power of true connection. My heart was always on my sleeve. But love has its own pace, and when it doesn't align, it leaves you learning in ways you never imagined.

Perhaps if the timing had been right, my story wouldn't just be about heartbreak—it might have been about triumph in love. Yet, here I am, still romantic, still writing, and maybe that's enough.

A Beautiful Paradox

He loved me. Or at least, he thought he did, with a madness that defied reason. I was his safe haven, the only one who could calm his storms, the only voice he ever truly listened to. In his eyes, I was irreplaceable—the one person he could trust, lean on, and surrender his vulnerabilities to. His love was intense, consuming, and, at times, breathtakingly beautiful. His love for me was undeniable and passionate, a force that could make the world feel right in an instant. But as deeply as he loved me, the mistreatment and the abuse began to overshadow that love, turning what should have been a haven into a battlefield. No matter how deeply he adored me or how fiercely he held on, it could never justify the moments that broke me. Love like that should have set us free, but instead, it chained me to the pain I never deserved.

The most painful part wasn't the arguments or the moments of uncertainty—it was the question that lingered at the back of my mind: *Did he ever truly love me? Or was that just his way of showing love?* The thought of loving someone with all my heart, yet never truly knowing if they felt the same, left me with a hollow ache. The never-ending question of whether what I thought was love was merely a reflection of what he knew or what he wanted to believe.

Some might call it *dilulu*, but I prefer to call it giving the benefit of the doubt—that maybe, just maybe, it was the only way he knew how to love. The pain, the words, the disrespect—I wasn't blind to them; I just convinced myself that it was all part of the package of love. Perhaps, in some twisted way, he had never been shown love in a healthier form. Maybe it was his own trauma, his own insecurities, that turned love into something else entirely—something toxic that I unknowingly embraced.

But still, in those moments, I couldn't hate him. I didn't know how to. The emotional scars may have been left behind, but love, for me, has always been a powerful force—so powerful that I could make excuses, overlook flaws, and try to understand the chaos.

Many believed I would write a romantic autobiography one day, one that could stretch across ten volumes, all about my love story. And truth be told, I probably talked about it that much in the past. A stranger would know my partner's name before mine—that's how I introduced myself. *On cloud nine, all the time.*

But here's the twist—it wasn't because I was always happy or fulfilled. This *unconditional love* I spoke of was, in truth, a veil to mask the hurt I didn't know how to unravel. I was deeply in pain but didn't know how to unlove.

People still ask me how I could not hate my partner after everything—the disrespect, being dragged on the floor, the manipulation when I was young, the verbal and physical abuse. Even now, my answer remains the same—I never learned how to unlove, or perhaps the fear rooted deep within me wouldn't allow it. But that fear is a story of its own, and this book isn't about that.

The most I could do was numb myself and bury those moments deep, never speaking of them again. But that silence? That was my cry for help, the only way I knew how to express the depths of what I had endured. Not talking about it didn't mean it didn't hurt—it meant I didn't have the words to explain. Hating him, or anyone for that matter doesn't feel natural to me. It's not who I am.

Though I dared to make this big move, a soft corner in my heart still remained for the relationship I had built, even as it bled and hurt me every day. It wasn't easy to give that up. I always believed that giving up was wrong, but over time, I learned that sometimes, holding on can be even more damaging.

You have to know when to let things go when to stop fantasizing about what *could be,* and when to accept the reality of *what is.* It took time, but I understood that letting go isn't a sign of weakness—it's a sign of strength and, sometimes, the only way to truly heal.

Love from Afar

It wasn't even a choice between loving or letting go—it was a choice between two kinds of pain. Letting go felt devastating, but staying and hoping for a different outcome was a whole different kind of suffering. Both paths looked like a constant, unrelenting ache, but when I finally let go, I gained something I didn't expect: the freedom to love unconditionally without needing to express it in words. And if I wanted to stay alive, I had no choice but to walk away from a relationship that was breaking me.

First, felt like a defense mechanism—an attempt to make sense of my pain and protect myself from experiencing it again. But as time passed, it transformed into something deeper, a spiritual unfolding that reshaped how I saw myself and the world around me. And so, my path to healing began—not by forgetting the past, but by truly understanding who I was. It was about peeling away the layers shaped by experiences, expectations, and fears and uncovering the self that existed beyond all of it. And in that search for myself, I turned inward.

If the world around me had shaped my fears and doubts, then only by looking within could I uncover the truth of who I really was. This was where my spiritual journey began anew—not in books or teachings, but in the quiet, unfiltered conversations I had with my own soul.

Chapter 1

The Mirror Within

Part 1

For as long as I can remember, I've analyzed my actions, words, and feelings with curiosity. While others might label this as overthinking, I've always seen it differently. Overthinking often carries the weight of anxiety—a relentless dwelling on *what could go wrong.* But self-introspection? That feels like peeling back the layers of my own being, understanding not just the *what* but the *why* behind my actions and reactions.

When I first started practicing self-introspection, it was largely reactive. I would analyze moments when I felt hurt, misunderstood, or angry. Self-awareness, at the time, was simply about identifying where I had gone wrong or how I could improve. But then, I realized self-awareness isn't just a tool for fixing mistakes; it's a bridge to understanding the fullness of life—my experiences, emotions, and relationships.

Gradually, Self-awareness taught me to focus less on the situation and more on how it shaped me.

It shifted my attention from external reactions to internal responses. *How did I feel? Why did I react the way I did? And most importantly, what lessons could I draw from these experiences to carry forward?*

I began to realize that the world often mirrors what lies within us. The way I respond to a challenge, the way I interpret a compliment, and even the way I navigate conflict all begin with me. When I observe these patterns with honesty and compassion, I uncover who I am now and who I have the potential to become.

And then there's the question that still lingers in the background: *Who am I?* Not just my name or my roles in life but the essence of *me*—my purpose, my values, and my lessons. Is there truly a grand purpose for each of us? Or is this search for purpose an elaborate illusion we've created to make sense of our existence?

I don't have all the answers yet, and perhaps I never will. This question isn't one to be answered in a single moment—it's a lifelong journey. Each day, each choice and each reflection adds another piece to the puzzle. Though it doesn't promise instant clarity or a neatly wrapped conclusion, it offers a sense of direction—a compass pointing inward, urging us to explore the depths of our hearts and minds. It reminds us that the answers we seek aren't *out there* in the world but within us, waiting to be discovered.

And when that happens, you will fall in love with yourself—not in a selfish, narcissistic way or to the extent that too much self-awareness hinders your ability to act naturally or take risks—but in a way that fosters pure respect, belief, and love for yourself, the universe, and others. But knowing how much is *too much* can be tricky; and that, I believe, is where spirituality plays a role.

Part 2: The First Step to Spirituality—Self-Awareness

The first step a spiritual seeker consciously takes is self-awareness. Spirituality, in its most profound sense, is a journey inward, and to embark on that path, a person must first develop an acute awareness of their inner thoughts, emotions, behaviors, and responses. This conscious awareness is not merely passive observation but an active engagement with oneself—a practice of noticing, questioning, and transforming.

In the *Bhagavad Gita*, Chapter 6, Verse 5, Krishna says:

"One must elevate, not degrade, oneself with one's mind. The mind is the friend of the conditioned soul and his enemy."

Self-awareness begins with the mastery of the mind. By observing and controlling the fluctuations of our thoughts, a spiritual person can learn to transcend ego-driven impulses. In this way, Krishna emphasizes that understanding the mind and gaining mastery over it is a critical step in one's spiritual development.

In this chapter, we will focus on *observing* our thoughts. *Controlling* the fluctuations of our thoughts and actions is a significant topic that we will discuss in the next chapter.

(The "Bhagavad Gita," or "Song of the Lord," is an 18-chapter dialogue between Krishna, the Lord of the Universe, and the warrior hero Arjuna.)

The Buddha often spoke about mindfulness in his teachings. In the *Satipatthana Sutta*, he emphasized the importance of cultivating awareness in every moment, particularly in relation to the body, feelings, mind, and mental objects. The Buddha's approach to self-awareness begins with body awareness, encouraging practitioners to feel their breath, movements, and sensations. By becoming deeply attuned to the present moment, one begins to understand the fleeting nature of thoughts, emotions, and physical sensations—all of which arise and pass away.

In the same *sutta*, the Buddha advises mindfulness of the mind:

"I will know whether my mind is with greed, hatred, delusion, or free from them."

Self-awareness in Buddhism involves recognizing the nature of one's thoughts—whether clouded by negative emotions such as greed or hatred or calm and free of mental afflictions. Through this practice, one can develop mental clarity and gradually purify the mind from unwholesome tendencies.

So, as we embark on this journey together, I invite you to take that first step. *Pause. Reflect. Ask yourself the hard questions.* Because the more you learn about who you are, the closer you'll come to understanding why you're here.

Suffering might seem inevitable, especially when considering spiritual concepts like karma, which we will explore as we go deeper. Still, the *Eightfold Path*, as taught by the Buddha, serves as a universal guide to liberating oneself from suffering. Self-awareness is crucial to every aspect of the path:

- Right View

- Right Intention

- Right Speech

- Right Action

- Right Livelihood

- Right Effort

- Right Mindfulness

- Right Concentration

These eight practices are not exclusive but serve as guiding principles for people from all walks of life, helping them become more aware of their thoughts, words, and actions while fostering ethical conduct, mental discipline, and wisdom.

The Eight Factors of the Noble Eightfold Path

1. Right View (Samma Ditthi)

Right View, the first factor of the Noble Eightfold Path, is crucial to understanding the nature of suffering and its cessation. It involves seeing things as they are and recognizing that attachment, craving, and ignorance are the root causes of suffering. This understanding enlightens us and encourages awareness of impermanence, suffering, and the interconnection of all things.

Key Lesson: The first step in any spiritual path is understanding the true nature of life and the mind. Right View encourages an awareness of impermanence, suffering, and the interconnection of all things.

2. Right Intention (Samma Sankappa)

Right Intention is the mental aspect of the path. It involves cultivating thoughts of renunciation, non-violence, and compassion while striving to free oneself from desires rooted in greed, hatred, and delusion.

Key Lesson: Our intentions shape our actions. By fostering pure, compassionate intentions, we align ourselves with a path of peace and enlightenment. This involves letting go of ego-driven desires and embracing kindness and wisdom.

3. Right Speech (Samma Vaca)

Right Speech encourages honesty, kindness, and mindfulness in communication. It involves abstaining from lying, gossiping, harsh speech, and divisive words.

Key Lesson: Words are powerful tools that can heal or harm. Right Speech requires us to speak truthfully and kindly, ensuring our words do not cause pain or misunderstanding. By practicing mindful speech, we create harmony around us.

4. Right Action (Samma Kammanta)

Right Action focuses on ethical conduct and refraining from actions that cause harm to oneself or others. This includes avoiding killing, stealing, and sexual misconduct.

Key Lesson: Our actions have consequences. Right Action guides us to live ethically, ensuring our conduct aligns with values of respect and compassion. It teaches us that we can create good karma through our daily choices.

5. Right Livelihood (Samma Ajiva)

Right Livelihood refers to choosing a profession or lifestyle that does not harm or exploit others. It involves earning a living ethically and honestly in a way that benefits both oneself and society.

Key Lesson: Our work should align with ethical principles, promoting well-being and respect for all living beings. Right Livelihood reminds us that we can stay true to our spiritual values even in our material pursuits.

6. Right Effort (Samma Vayama)

Right Effort is the continuous practice of eliminating unwholesome qualities and cultivating wholesome ones. It involves avoiding negative mental states such as anger and jealousy and instead nurturing states like loving-kindness, patience, and joy.

Key Lesson: Change requires effort. By cultivating good habits and abandoning harmful ones, we gradually transform our minds. Right Effort encourages persistence in our spiritual practice, knowing that growth takes time.

7. Right Mindfulness (Samma Sati)

Right Mindfulness involves developing awareness and attention in every moment. It teaches us to observe the body, feelings, mind, and mental objects without attachment or aversion.

Key Lesson: Being mindful means being aware of our thoughts, emotions, and actions in each moment. Through mindfulness, we see the impermanent nature of everything and learn to let go of attachments that cause suffering.

8. Right Concentration (Samma Samadhi)

Right Concentration refers to the practice of meditation, where one cultivates a focused and calm mind. Through deep concentration, one can attain higher states of meditation and insight, leading to wisdom and liberation from suffering.

Key Lesson: The mind is often scattered, but through meditation and concentration, we develop clarity and insight. Right Concentration enables us to deepen our understanding of reality and achieve inner peace.

A spiritually aware person understands that life's challenges are opportunities for growth. They observe their thoughts and emotions with detachment, aligning their actions with higher principles. The lessons from Krishna and Buddha remind us that self-awareness is not just about understanding who we are but also about recognizing our interconnectedness with all beings and the divine essence that binds us.

The *Bhagavad Gita* and the Buddha's teachings agree that self-awareness is a lifelong journey requiring mindfulness, discipline, and reflection. Krishna's emphasis on detachment aligns with the Buddha's principle of non-attachment. Both highlight the need to rise above the ego and temporary desires to discover the eternal truth within.

In modern spiritual practices, this journey begins with mindfulness. Whether through meditation, prayer, journaling, breath observation, or simple reflection, the goal is to slow down and observe the mind, body, and soul. Only when we see ourselves clearly can we make deliberate changes in our lives.

Looking back at my experiences, I see how much I've been forced to confront—not just the challenges life has thrown at me but also the ones I've unknowingly created for myself. Moving abroad, adjusting to the harsh realities of immigrant life, and dealing with heartbreak weren't just external struggles; they were invitations to understand deeper layers of myself.

At first, I didn't even recognize it as self-awareness when my mind replayed thoughts—not out of anxiety, but out of a need to understand, to find multiple perspectives in the situations I faced. While it may have felt like I was caught in a loop, I wasn't spiraling into depression. I was sifting through my emotions, my past, and the things that held me back, learning to process them rather than just pushing them aside. This awareness set me free.

As a spiritual seeker, it's humbling to realize that much of my journey unknowingly reflects the principles of Buddha's *Eightfold Path*. I didn't set out with this specific intention, but through the nurturing of those around me, I was drawn to qualities like Right Livelihood and Right Intention. However, the deeper I delve into the meaning of Right Action, the more I realize it's not just about how I treat others—it's also about how I treat myself.

For so long, I misunderstood the importance of self-care and self-compassion, often confusing them with selfishness.

This misunderstanding led me down a path of self-sacrifice, where I put everyone else's needs above my own, neglecting my well-being. Through journaling, meditation, and spending time with myself, I gained the clarity to recognize this imbalance.

If you are new to meditation, learning from a guru or teacher can be beneficial. While no one can make you meditate, a teacher can effectively guide you by explaining instructions and demonstrating proper posture. This guidance helps you develop a practice that you can eventually undertake on your own.

Journaling is one of my favorite activities. Whether I'm experiencing joy, sorrow, love, or strange dreams, my journal is a steadfast companion that captures these moments. This practice not only curbs the urge to overshare but also provides a sacred space for self-reflection.

My love for collecting journals eventually motivated me to create one. You can find my favorite plain and interactive journal books here: www.hastileo.com

If you are unsure about your position in the journey of self-discovery, consider using this simple guide: *The Four Self-Awareness Archetypes.*

The Four Self-Awareness Archetypes

In the journey of self-discovery, we exhibit traits that align with specific archetypes—representations of how we perceive ourselves and our interactions with the world. These archetypes reflect varying levels of internal awareness and external understanding, forming a framework to evaluate our relationship with the self and others. Here are **The Four Self-Awareness Archetypes**:

1. The Seeker

Characteristics:

- Driven by curiosity and a desire for growth.

- Often asks introspective questions: *Who am I? What is my purpose?*

- Open to learning from experiences, mistakes, and external feedback.

Strengths:

- Highly motivated to expand their understanding.

- Willing to explore new paths and confront discomfort to gain insight.

Challenges:

- May overanalyze or feel lost in the process of discovery.

- Tends to rely too heavily on external validation.

Example:

A person embarking on spiritual practices or therapy to uncover their inner truths falls into this archetype.

2. The Confident Realist

Characteristics:

- Possesses clarity about their strengths and limitations.

- Balances introspection with an understanding of how they affect others.

- Acts decisively based on an alignment of values and goals.

Strengths:

- Grounded and self-assured, yet open to feedback.

- Adept at fostering genuine connections with others.

Challenges:

- May face resistance from others who misinterpret their confidence as arrogance.

Example:

An individual who leads with authenticity embraces their imperfections and helps others without overshadowing their own needs.

3. The Introspective Dreamer

Characteristics:

- Deeply reflective and immersed in their inner world.

- Strong creative tendencies, often expressing their emotions through art, writing, or music.

- Focused on internal awareness but struggles to navigate external dynamics.

Strengths:

- Has a rich internal dialogue and deep emotional insight.

- Highly empathetic and sensitive to others' unspoken emotions.

Challenges:

- Can become withdrawn or disconnected from reality.

- They may struggle with overthinking or taking action.

Example:

A writer crafting poetry to process emotions but hesitant to share their work due to self-doubt.

4. The Reactive Observer

Characteristics:

- Primarily focused on external events and reactions.

- Less aware of internal emotions or the deeper motivations behind their actions.

- Tends to blame circumstances rather than seeking internal solutions.

Strengths:

- Keenly aware of external trends and dynamics.

- Good at adapting to changing situations.

Challenges:

- Lacks introspection, leading to repeated patterns of dissatisfaction.

- Struggles to recognize how internal beliefs shape external outcomes.

Example:

An individual who frequently changes jobs or relationships, attributing dissatisfaction to external factors without addressing underlying patterns.

Applying the Archetypes

These archetypes are not fixed categories but fluid states. You might find yourself transitioning between them at different phases of your life or in response to specific situations. The key is recognizing where you stand and using that awareness to evolve.

For example:

- A **Seeker** might grow into a **Confident Realist** through consistent reflection and action.

- An **Introspective Dreamer** could benefit from engaging more with external environments to balance their creativity with reality.

The goal is not to label but to identify your starting point and use it as a guide to nurture greater self-awareness and harmony.

Chapter 2

The Power of Self-Control

Self-control is the bridge that connects our current self with the person we are destined to become. It is the empowering force that enables us to transcend distractions, impulses, and the constant allure of desire. But self-control is not about harsh denial or leading a life of scarcity; rather, it is a conscious effort to direct our energies and actions in harmony with our deeper values.

On the spiritual journey, self-control is not just a tool—it is a pathway to liberation. It allows us to surpass the limitations of the ego and step into the fullness of our potential, granting us a sense of freedom and independence.

In many ways, self-control is about creating space for our higher self to express itself. When we cultivate control over our thoughts, emotions, and actions, we allow deeper wisdom to arise.

When we let ourselves be swept away by impulses, we lose touch with our true essence. The mind becomes a chaotic storm of thoughts and desires, pulling us in every direction. Self-control, however, is the anchor that stabilizes us. Discipline allows us to pause, reflect, and choose our actions consciously rather than reacting impulsively. As we master our actions, we begin to experience the peace of stillness. The more we control both our external and internal worlds, the more we cultivate a sense of calm and tranquility.

Krishna's Wisdom on Self-Control

In the *Bhagavad Gita*, Krishna closely links self-control with devotion. For Krishna, authentic yogic practice is not just about physical postures or rituals but about learning to master the mind through self-discipline. He says:

"The mind is restless, turbulent, strong, and obstinate; but by practice and detachment, it can be controlled."

This is where self-control becomes a vital tool in our spiritual journey. Through conscious practice and the willingness to let go of attachments, we create the conditions for spiritual awakening.

The Buddha's Teachings: The Path of Mindful Control

The Buddha also emphasized the necessity of self-control on the path to enlightenment. In his teachings on the *Noble Eightfold Path*, mindfulness plays an integral role in cultivating self-discipline. Right Effort, Right Mindfulness, and Right

Concentration all point toward the importance of controlling the mind and emotions in a way that leads us closer to freedom.

The Daily Practice of Self-Control

Self-control is not about renouncing pleasure or material comforts; rather, it is about recognizing the impermanence of all things and choosing to engage with them from a place of inner peace rather than craving.

The beauty of self-control is that it is a practice we can cultivate in every moment. It is not an all-or-nothing concept but a gradual, unfolding process of learning and refining ourselves. Every day presents opportunities to practice—whether in our thoughts, speech, or actions. The true beauty lies in the transformation it brings, the empowerment it offers, and the peace it instills in our lives.

For instance, when we feel the urge to react impulsively in a challenging situation, self-control invites us to pause, take a breath, and respond with clarity. When tempted by desires that do not serve our highest good, it teaches us to observe the impulse without acting on it, understanding that we are not our desires but the observers of them. This subtle shift in awareness allows us to make choices that reflect our higher values and long-term goals.

The path can be challenging. There will be moments when we stumble, when our desires or emotions overwhelm us. However, it is essential to remember that self-control is not about perfection but progress. Small, everyday choices—like resisting the urge to check your phone during a conversation, choosing a healthy meal over fast food, or refraining from gossip—are all opportunities to cultivate self-discipline.

The Fruits of Self-Control

The rewards of self-control are profound. By mastering ourselves, we begin to experience the fruits of spiritual growth—peace, wisdom, and inner freedom. As we cultivate self-control, we become less reactive to the external world and more attuned to our inner truth. We come to understand that true happiness is not found in external circumstances but in inner peace.

Self-control also strengthens our relationships. When we regulate our impulses and reactions, we can respond to others with greater compassion, patience, and understanding. We engage in relationships from a place of love rather than neediness, offering support and kindness without attachment.

In this way, self-control not only serves our personal growth but also enhances our ability to contribute positively to the world.

Looking back, I can see that my journey has been one of constant choice and restraint. The path to self-control has not been easy; it has required me to confront my desires, emotions, and instincts. It has been about learning when to push forward and when to step back. For me, self-control wasn't about suppression or denial but about balance. It was about understanding that not everything needed to be reacted to immediately and that sometimes, the most powerful thing I could do was to pause and reflect before making a decision.

I've often been someone who gives a lot of myself to others emotionally—and for a long time, I believed this was the right way to be. But through my journey, I've realized that I need to exercise self-control in how much I give. I've learned to set boundaries, say *no* when needed, and protect my energy. This wasn't an easy lesson. It meant having to face my fears of guilt and disappointment. But each time I chose to prioritize my well-being, I realized it wasn't selfish—it was a necessary act of self-respect.

A pivotal moment in my practice of self-control came when I faced the heartbreak that had once defined so much of my emotional landscape. When I finally decided to stop communicating with my partner and ignored the countless calls that followed, it took immense self-control. Despite the love I still felt and my longing for answers, I resisted the urge to reach out. Every instinct urged me to pick up the phone, explain everything, and relive the connection we once shared. However, I knew that doing so would only entrap me further in a cycle of reactions.

In the past, I would have been consumed by the pain, reacting impulsively, seeking distractions, or even trying to force closure when I wasn't ready. But this time, I practiced self-control. I allowed myself to grieve. I didn't let it drive me into unhealthy patterns of behavior. Instead, I permitted myself to feel what I needed to feel and then consciously chose to heal. This was perhaps the most significant lesson in self-control I have learned—choosing not to let my circumstances control my reactions.

I began with the most challenging step: controlling the emotion of love. Love, as powerful and beautiful as it is, can also be blinding. I stopped expressing the depth of my feelings because I realized they were no longer met with the same honesty or respect. When love is unreciprocated or undervalued, it becomes a burden rather than a joy.

I didn't stop loving; I stopped giving my love to someone who did not know how to handle it. Trust me, it's not as easy as it sounds, especially when you have so much love to give and are *not reacting*. My growing spiritual journey illuminated the reality I had been blind to for so long. Self-control became my weapon of liberation. It was the key to breaking free from the cycle that held me back.

Next came anger—the second storm I had to tame. Controlling my emotions was just one part of my journey; the other—perhaps the most transformative aspect—was learning to manage my reactions when triggered.

For years, people have used my expressions of love or responses in anger to their benefit. For years, I allowed my anger to be provoked. It was easy for my partner, or even the world around me, to push the buttons that set me off. My reactions gave others power over me—power they did not deserve.

The shift began when I understood that my anger was mine to control, not theirs to manipulate.

Now, when someone tries to provoke me, I take a deep breath—a small act with immense power. That breath anchors me in the present and reminds me of my strength. At that moment, as I exhale, I release not just air, but also the control they once had over me. That breath serves as my boundary, my silent declaration that their tricks or manipulations will not sway me.

This transformation was not simply about suppressing my anger but about reclaiming my peace.

Unleashed anger destroys clarity, but controlled anger can fuel change.

Misplaced love drains the soul, but love toward oneself becomes the foundation of strength.

Self-control didn't just save me; it empowered me. It enabled me to walk away from toxic patterns without bitterness, to protect my energy without guilt, and to stand tall without being drawn into the chaos that others create.

This chapter of my life is not merely about controlling emotions or reactions. It's about understanding that self-control is the foundation of freedom. It deepens with every experience, challenge, and moment of reflection. As I continue on this journey, I realize that self-control is not something I master once and for all. It's an ongoing practice, a continual process of tuning in to myself, checking my impulses, and acting in ways that reflect the person I am becoming. In this practice, I find freedom—not the kind of freedom that comes from doing whatever I want, but the more profound freedom that comes from knowing I can choose my path, actions, and responses.

Through self-control, we come to understand that our desires do not define us but by our ability to rise above them, act with wisdom, and live in harmony with the greater whole.

Chapter 3

Mindful Speaking: The Balance Between Words and Silence

In today's world, we often categorize people as introverts or extroverts based on how they interact with others. However, this classification overlooks a deeper aspect of human behavior — the ability to engage in mindful speaking. Mindful speaking is not just about being extroverted or introverted. It's about being aware of your words' impact on yourself and others.

Introverts might stay silent because they value reflection and inner peace, while extroverts might be more vocal and seek connection through words. But the common thread here is mindfulness —the ability to speak consciously and with intention and to listen to the wisdom of silence when necessary. By reframing introversion and extroversion as mindful speaking, we empower ourselves to communicate with intention, understanding the weight of our words and the power of silence.

For me, mindfulness in speaking means being aware of how my words affect my state of mind and the atmosphere around me.

It's about understanding that words are not just fleeting sounds; they carry the power to create, destroy, and build connections or distance. In my earlier years, I would express every feeling, no matter the consequences, because I believed it was better to let it out than to let it fester inside. Over time, I've learned that not every thought needs to be expressed. Embracing silence can often be the most potent form of communication. Just as I have learned to respect the divine within myself, I value each word I speak. It's a practice of self-awareness, recognizing when to speak and when silence is the most effective response. This understanding did not come easily, but it arrived at the right time.

My family used to tease me about my chatterbox days, but now they see that my quieter moments reflect my growth journey. While they were initially concerned, they've embraced this evolution. I'm excited to share the insights I've gained along the way!

Staying silent brings a lot of benefits, both spiritually and mentally. Here are some key benefits of embracing silence:

Mental Clarity: Silence clears the mind, helping you organize thoughts and gain clarity.

Emotional Healing: Silence provides space to process emotions, fostering inner healing.

Stress Reduction: Quiet moments calm the nervous system, lowering stress and anxiety.

Improved Focus: Silence sharpens concentration, boosting productivity and efficiency.

Deeper Connections: Active silence helps you listen deeply, strengthening relationships.

Self-Awareness: Silence encourages introspection, enhancing self-understanding and growth.

Spiritual Growth: It opens a gateway to spiritual practices, fostering inner peace and connection.

Creative Flow: Silence stimulates creativity by allowing ideas to emerge freely.

Intentional Communication: Speaking less makes words more impactful, promoting thoughtful dialogue.

Patience and Tolerance: Silence cultivates patience, allowing you to respond with greater tolerance.

Spiritual essence:

In **Dhammapada** (a collection of sayings of the Buddha), several verses highlight the importance of silence:

"Better than a thousand hollow words is one word that brings peace." (Dhammapada 100)

This quote speaks to the power of speaking with intention—choosing words that create peace rather than more noise and disturbance.

Noble Silence in Buddhism is often about cultivating deep awareness, transcending superficial chatter, and cultivating mindfulness in speech and action. In the **Vinaya Pitaka**, Buddha speaks about "right speech"—avoiding gossip, lying, or harmful words, which leads to inner peace and harmony. Buddha also teaches that true silence comes from within and is a practice of inner stillness and mind control.

As The Bible verse Proverbs 17:27 says, "The one who knows much says little; an understanding person remains calm." This verse suggests that a wise person knows when to speak and uses words with restraint. The verse suggests that a wise person is careful with their words. It's not just what we say but how and when we say it.

Chapter 4

Solitude: A Sacred Space

In a world that constantly encourages social connection, solitude can be viewed with hesitation or fear. Yet, when embraced with intention, solitude has the transformative power to become one of our greatest allies. In these quiet moments, we can tap into profound personal strength and spiritual growth, uncovering truths about ourselves that may have otherwise remained hidden.

From a spiritual perspective, solitude is not just about being physically alone; it's about creating space to connect with your deeper self beyond the world's noise. It allows us to return to our inner essence, reconnect with the divine within us, and reorient ourselves toward the truth of our being.

I had always been pampered to the core. My family ensured I was cared for in every possible way, even as I transitioned into adulthood. I don't recall a day when I had to eat all three meals alone. My brother fed me breakfast and dinner, while every lunch during college was hand-fed to me, often by my partner. Despite the turbulence and disrespect in that relationship, this remains a tender memory I will cherish forever.

I had never experienced life away from the comforts of home—no hostel stays, no overnights at a cousin's or friend's place. My family was always nearby, wrapping me in a cocoon of love and care. But when it was time for me to move, my family? They didn't flinch. They knew me better. They knew the fire beneath the softness, the quiet determination behind the delicate exterior. They had seen me fight for what I wanted, love with all my heart, and work harder than anyone expected. And they trusted me to take on the world—even if that world was thousands of miles away.

With no contact support system and a suitcase of dreams, I landed in the United States, only to learn that the world had shut down for COVID-19. While the pandemic brought devastation and unimaginable loss to so many, for which my heart aches, it unexpectedly offered me a chance to pause and reflect. The lockdown became a time for deep introspection and personal growth, a privilege I don't take lightly.

As the world battled feelings of isolation and loneliness, I discovered something powerful—I thrived in it. For someone who always believed that solitude is strength, this was my chance to prove it. There was no familiar hum of family life, no social distractions—just me, my thoughts, and the freedom to shape my days. The silence wasn't a void but a canvas to rediscover myself.

I found clarity, resilience, and a renewed sense of purpose in solitude.

I love being alone for two main reasons:

Reclaiming Personal Power

In solitude, we can reclaim our power. It is easy to give away our energy in relationships, work, and other commitments, often to the point of exhaustion. Solitude allows us to replenish our reserves, regain our emotional energy, and return to the world stronger. In this stillness, we reconnect with our inner strength and remind ourselves of our inherent worth, regardless of external circumstances.

Buddha's teachings about detachment emphasize the importance of standing in our power, free from the need for validation from others. Solitude offers the perfect space for this reclamation.

Connecting to the Divine

Solitude is also a doorway to spiritual connection. Whether through prayer, meditation, or quiet contemplation, being alone deepens our connection with the divine. We often find the most profound spiritual insights in the silent space created by solitude.

In the *Gita*, Krishna urges Arjuna to seek refuge in him and trust in his divine plan. In moments of solitude, we, too, can surrender our worries, open ourselves to divine guidance, and experience the profound peace of knowing we are part of something greater than ourselves.

With a foundation deeply rooted in spirituality, I embraced it anew—this time with conscious intent. Spirituality was no longer just a part of my upbringing but a deliberate choice, a guiding light that brought clarity and calm to life's uncertainties.

Chapter 5

God is fair

Though my life has often felt like a rollercoaster, filled with twists and turns I had little control over, the environment I grew up in instilled a deep belief in God. That belief was solidified not just through teachings or rituals but through my own experiences— moments where I felt the presence of something greater guiding me. I believe in God wholeheartedly, and for those around me, I often say, *"God is fair."*

What I find difficult to accept, however, is the negativity that arises when people become jealous of others' lives. It pains me to see individuals walking around envious of someone else's bare minimum instead of appreciating the blessings they've been given. We each have our unique mix of blessings and challenges, carefully balanced in ways we may not immediately understand. When embraced and overcome, challenges often turn into our greatest strengths.

But jealousy clouds that perspective. Instead of passing negative energy or undermining others, why not take a moment to count your blessings? It could be as simple as the meal on your plate, the healthy body that allows you to enjoy it, or the means to afford it. These are all reasons to be grateful. Gratitude is a powerful antidote to envy—it shifts your focus from what others have to what you already possess.

When we truly appreciate our journey, we naturally exude positive energy, lifting ourselves and those around us. In doing so, we align with God's fairness, who has given each of us exactly what we need to thrive in our unique way.

If you do not believe in God, I will not judge you. Your beliefs are your own, and I respect that.

A Lesson from My Yoga Teacher

It was a pleasant morning in class, and as always, my yoga teacher, Austin Sanderson, began the session by chanting a mantra. Each word was carefully explained, unraveling layers of meaning, I had never considered. That day, he delved into the concept of believing in God, emphasizing how deeply personal and unique this belief can be, shaped by one's individual experiences and circumstances.

While I may not have his eloquence in explaining such profound ideas, I can share what resonated with me.

For someone born in a place where survival is a daily battle, where people must walk miles just to fetch a mug of water, the idea of God might emerge as something to fear—a force to be appeased lest it withholds even the bare essentials. On the other hand, for someone whose life overflows with abundance and security, God might be seen as a source of grace or the supreme creator deserving of gratitude.

These interpretations are not right or wrong—they reflect lived realities. My teacher helped me see that belief in God is not about rigid definitions but about alignment and perspective. It is molded by our struggles, joys, and everything in between. That realization shifted my understanding of faith—it is less about the form God takes and more about the relationship we choose to have with the divine based on our unique journeys.

Whether we see God as a force to fear, a savior to lean on, or an essence to revere, our journey is valid and respected.

My Experience

I have never been one to harbor jealousy, even in the face of significant challenges like turbulent relationships or financial struggles. It's not because my life has been without hardship but because I've seen those challenges as stepping stones rather than stumbling blocks. No matter how daunting, every obstacle has been a lesson in disguise—a push toward growth, resilience, and self-awareness.

Sometimes, I observed friends seemingly enjoying life to the fullest while I found myself entangled in family challenges. It could have been easy to feel envious, to question why some seem to walk a lighter path while others carry heavier burdens. But instead of dwelling on comparisons, I chose to see it differently. I began asking, *What is this experience meant to teach me?*

This perspective helped me recognize that everyone fights battles we cannot see—struggles are often hidden behind the smiles they share with the world. Those moments of laughter and joy, however fleeting, are precious. They serve as a sanctuary from pain, a reminder that happiness can coexist with hardship.

In those moments, I realized the power of kindness. Contributing to someone else's happiness, even in small ways, can create ripples of positivity that stretch far beyond what we see. Simply being genuinely happy for others or adding to their joy costs nothing, yet it has the potential to uplift us all. It's a reminder that life isn't about comparison but about connection, understanding, and the shared humanity that binds us.

As for me, trusting in God gives me the strength to endure. If I experience pain today, I choose to believe it's a preparation for the joy that is yet to come. Every hardship is like the dark before dawn, a prerequisite to understanding and appreciating the light. After all, God is fair. He knows what each of us needs and when we need it. This trust in His timing allows me to face life's challenges with grace and gratitude. My struggles are ultimately for my good, paving the way for a stronger, wiser version of myself. Instead of dwelling on what I lack or what others have, I focus on the blessings I've been given. There is power in gratitude, in counting the good days I've had amidst the storms. Envying another's journey is to undermine my unique purpose. With all its twists and turns, my path is mine to walk—and I wouldn't trade it for anything.

Chapter 6

Divine Balance

Seeing the Divine in Others While Neglecting the Divine Within

One of the most subtle yet profound lessons I've learned on my journey is the delicate balance between seeing the divine spark in others and honoring the divine within myself. It's a spiritual paradox that many of us face. On the one hand, we are encouraged to see the *atman*—the divine soul—in everyone, recognizing that we are all connected and part of the same universal consciousness. On the other hand, in our eagerness to uplift and serve others, we often forget to nurture the divine essence within ourselves.

In my life, this imbalance played out in ways that I didn't recognize until much later. I devoted so much energy to seeing the good in others, understanding their struggles, and empathizing with their pain that I neglected to extend the same love and understanding to myself. I thought that by focusing on others, I was being selfless and spiritual. But over time, I realized that true spirituality isn't about losing yourself in others—it's about maintaining the harmony between giving and receiving, and honoring others *and* yourself.

Recognizing the Divine in Others

The *Bhagavad Gita* teaches us to see the *atman* in all beings. This is a powerful practice because it shifts our perspective from judgment to compassion. When we view others as extensions of the divine, we stop seeing them as separate from us. We begin to appreciate their struggles, forgive their flaws, and celebrate their victories as if they were our own.

This mindset has been transformative for me. It has helped me build deeper connections and see the beauty in even the most challenging relationships. It's why I could empathize with people who hurt me, understanding that their actions often came from their pain. It's why I could give endlessly, even when it cost me peace.

But therein lay the problem—I was so focused on recognizing the divine in others that I ignored the divine within me.

The *atman*, the eternal soul, resides in each of us. It's our true self, beyond the body and mind, and it's just as sacred as the divine spark we see in others. Yet, in my desire to be kind, understanding, and selfless, I often neglected to listen to my own soul. I accepted mistreatment because I believed it was my duty to be patient and forgiving. I gave more than I could afford—emotionally, mentally, and physically—because I thought it was the "right" thing to do. I silenced my own needs because I believed they were less important than the needs of others.

But the truth is, when we neglect the divine within us, we dishonor the very source of our being. The *Gita* doesn't ask us to see the divine in others at the expense of ourselves. It teaches us to recognize that same divinity in all beings, *including ourselves.*

Finding Balance

Finding the balance between honoring others and yourself is not easy, especially if you've spent years prioritizing others over yourself. It requires you to unlearn the belief that self-care is selfish and replace it with the understanding that self-care is sacred.

This shift began when I realized that the love and compassion I extended to others were incomplete if I couldn't extend the same to myself. *How could I truly see the divine in others if I ignored it within myself? How could I uplift others if I was constantly running on empty?*

I started small. I set boundaries—not as walls to keep people out but as bridges to maintain my own balance. I began to listen to my inner voice, honor my intuition, and trust that my feelings and needs were valid. I learned to say *no* without guilt, understanding that it was an act of self-respect. Most importantly, I began to see myself as worthy of the same love and understanding I gave to others.

This wasn't easy—it required me to confront the fears and insecurities that had kept me in a cycle of self-neglect. But with time, I realized that by honoring myself, I was nurturing my soul and creating a stronger foundation from which to serve others.

As I continue to walk this path, I remind myself daily that seeing the divine in others and honoring the divine within are not opposing practices—they are two sides of the same coin. Together, they create a life of harmony, purpose, and peace.

Chapter 7

Everything Happens at the Right Time: A Personal Reflection on Divine Timing

The concept of timing has always intrigued me, especially when reflecting on my life journey. The idea that things unfold in their own time—not according to our desires but according to divine orchestration—has become a source of deep comfort.

As the *Bhagavad Gita* teaches, we should surrender to the divine will and trust in the timing of events. In Chapter 2, Verse 47, Krishna speaks to Arjuna:

"You have the right to perform your prescribed duties, but you are not entitled to the fruits of your actions. Never consider yourself to be the cause of the results of your activities, nor be attached to inaction."

In this context, Krishna advises Arjuna (and us, as readers) to act with complete sincerity and dedication to our duties without being overly concerned about when or how the results will manifest.

We have the right to perform our duties, but the outcomes are shaped by more than just our actions.

Many factors influence the results—our efforts, the weight of destiny shaped by past *karmas*, divine will, the contributions of others, collective *karmas*, and even the circumstances and timing that might seem like mere chance. When we become overly attached to the results, we allow anxiety to take root, especially when outcomes don't align with our expectations. By letting go of the need to control results, we free ourselves from unnecessary stress and distractions.

The lesson here is that by focusing on the right action at the right time—doing our duty in the present moment—we align with the flow of the universe, which will naturally bring the outcomes at the right time, even if we cannot foresee them. The emphasis on not being attached to the fruits of our actions also suggests that the results are not under our control but part of a larger, divine plan that unfolds at the right time.

I remember a time in my life when I wanted things to happen urgently. I was so eager for change, growth, and answers to questions that had lingered in my heart for years. But in those moments, I realized that my impatience was the barrier to my progress.

I had forgotten that the journey itself was a part of the timing I had to trust.

Things started falling into place when I surrendered my attachment to a specific timeline. This experience made me reflect on Krishna's teachings more deeply: there is no need to rush; everything will unfold in its own time as long as I stay true to my path.

Similarly, in the **Bible**, the story of timing is beautifully encapsulated in the well-known verse from

Ecclesiastes 3:1: *"To everything, there is a season, a time for every purpose under heaven."* This verse suggests that life has its rhythm, and sometimes, we must pause, reflect, and recognize that not everything is within our control. Ecclesiastes 3:1 is part of a passage that lists many different seasons, including birth, death, planting, uprooting, killing, healing, tearing down, building, weeping, laughing, mourning, dancing, scattering stones, gathering stones, embracing, refraining from embracing, seeking, losing, keeping, sewing, being silent, speaking, loving, hating, war, and peace. Whatever God takes us through has a purpose, perhaps to deepen our faith or to help us achieve a breakthrough in an area of life.

Psalm 27:14 – "Wait for the Lord; be strong and take heart and wait for the Lord." This verse highlights the importance of waiting on God's perfect timing and finding strength and courage in that waiting.

Romans 8:28 – "And we know that in all things God works for the good of those who love him, who have been called according to his purpose." This assures us that even when things don't go according to our timeline, God is still at work in our lives, orchestrating everything for our good.

Whether the Bhagavad Gita's spiritual wisdom or the Bible's practical wisdom, both remind me that everything happens at the right time. The key is to trust in that divine timing—believing that a more fantastic plan is far beyond what I can comprehend now. Through this trust, I've found peace, even in moments of waiting. It's not easy to stay, but when I look back at the pieces of my life, I see the beauty in how they came together, each event perfectly timed, and each lesson learned when I was ready to receive it. I've realized that things happen not when I demand them but when I am ready.

And that's my answer for everyone who asks about my marriage life now. A saying in Hindi, *"Samay se pehle, bhagya se adhik kuch nahi milta,"* translates to, "One gets nothing before the fated time and no more than one's fair share as destined."

The right circumstances, partner, and moments often arrive when we least expect them but exactly when they are meant to. Embracing this belief has been a source of comfort and strength, helping me navigate the uncertainties of life with greater acceptance. It's not that I never stress or worry—those moments are inevitable—but I've learned to cultivate calmness even amid chaos.

Finding Support in Unexpected Places

God sends the right people into our lives at the right moments. Unlike traditional joint families, my nuclear family of four relied solely on each other for support during both joyful and challenging times.

School was often a difficult experience due to impatient and rude teachers, which made me enjoy it less. Because of my father's changing job locations, we frequently moved around the city, requiring me to switch schools and make new friends each time. This transient lifestyle likely contributed to my having fewer friendships. Teachers at each new school treated me differently— some viewed teaching as merely a job rather than a passion.

I remember feeling particularly hurt when teachers were unkind to me simply because I was favored by a colleague they disliked.

These situations often placed me in an uncomfortable spotlight. However, a few of my teachers, especially those who taught mathematics and Kannada, quickly noticed the problem and took a stand for me.

It was then that I realized the problem wasn't me. Their encouragement helped me overcome my fear, rekindle my love for school, and instill in me a deep sense of gratitude and hope for the future. By the time I entered college, this newfound confidence had replaced any lingering doubt and fear. At the same time, I grew both bolder and more sensitive.

In college, I became quite popular. I made many good friends and earned numerous medals from intercollegiate competitions. My undergraduate years were filled with positive experiences that helped me distinguish between good opportunities and bad company.

Despite the challenges of frequently changing schools and dealing with unkind teachers, the support and encouragement from those few compassionate educators left a lasting impact on me. Their influence shaped my resilience and self-assurance, qualities that have been invaluable throughout my life. These experiences taught me that people enter our lives at the right time.

Even the relationship I had—though it brought more pain than peace—was all about timing. Had I not fallen into that relationship, I doubt I would have developed the confidence I have today. The experiences I faced forced me to confront my deepest fears and weaknesses, and it was through that struggle that I grew stronger. Without those challenges, I wouldn't have developed the empathy that now helps me serve as a life coach to hundreds of people who have faced similar emotional struggles.

Every person I've encountered—whether a flatmate, a leader early in my career, or even a stranger I met at the temple last month—has left an indelible mark on my journey. Each one has inspired me in their own way, contributing to my life and shaping the person I am today.

I remember when I refused to move abroad for my undergraduate studies despite my parents wanting me to. A second chance came when my life was in shambles—so far gone that I thought only a miracle, or perhaps God Himself, could pull me out of it. I had reached a point where my choices had led me to the edge, and there was no easy way back. This second chance wasn't just a lifeline; it was a matter of survival. I needed it like I needed air—a way to feel alive again and rediscover the person I had lost somewhere along the way.

This time, it felt like fate was extending its hand, offering me a chance to rewrite the story I had almost lost control of. All I had to do was trust, take a step forward, and grasp the opportunity.

And it all happened—not when I wanted, but when I needed it most. Looking back, I can see how perfect the timing was. Each encounter came at precisely the right moment, providing me with exactly what I needed—guidance, a challenge, or a lesson.

The key is to surrender. Surrendering to the flow of life doesn't mean giving up or being passive. It means trusting that we are exactly where we need to be, even if it doesn't look like what we expected.

Chapter 8

Getting easy on temporary

PEOPLE

Just as the people who enter our lives play a crucial role in shaping our growth, it's equally important to recognize when it's time for them to exit. Timing isn't just about arrivals; it's about departures, too. There's a profound lesson in understanding when a relationship has reached its natural conclusion, no matter how important it once was. Holding on to something past its time can drain us. The right people teach us, love us, and help us grow, but sometimes, they are meant to leave, making space for new lessons and growth. Understanding this truth and gracefully letting go has been one of the most empowering realizations of my life. It's not about bitterness or regret but about honoring their role in our journey while trusting that their exit is part of the divine timing guiding us forward. Letting go of the temporary is not about abandoning everything we value, but rather, it's about not letting these things dictate our happiness. One of the most freeing moments of my journey was learning to distinguish between temporary and permanent. The impermanence of life became apparent to me in the face of changing circumstances, losses, and challenges. Understanding that nothing lasts forever—relationships, success, or struggles - was liberating. When we stop defining ourselves by the temporary, we free ourselves from the constant cycle of gain and loss. We become more aligned with who we are, our true essence, which is not dependent on external factors.

This realization also helped me when it came to people. I've had relationships with friends and relatives that I held on to for far too long, not because I saw them as my source of happiness or security, but because I believed relationships were not meant to be broken. I would not give up, even when I was hurt. While I had enough self-respect not to reach out on my own, if the other person initiated a conversation, I would forgive them wholeheartedly, without regret or guilt, and move forward as if nothing had ever gone wrong between us. But in time, I learned that not every person is meant to stay in your life forever, and that's okay. Relationships are meaningful, but clinging to them despite pain can hinder growth. Forgiveness is noble, yet it's equally vital to recognize when a connection has run its course.

The more I embraced the impermanence of life, the more I realized that absolute freedom comes from within. It comes from letting go of the temporary distractions and focusing on what lasts—the soul's growth, the clarity of the mind, and the peace within. This is the essence of living freely, without the weight of attachment to anything or anyone.

MATERIALISTIC PLEASURES

In a world where the pursuit of more is often equated with success, it's easy to fall into the trap of believing that material possessions can provide lasting happiness. From the latest gadgets to a bigger house or a fancier car, we're often led to believe that the more we acquire, the more complete our lives will be. But, when we take a step back and genuinely reflect, we realize that while these possessions may bring temporary satisfaction, they don't bring lasting fulfillment.

The constant cycle of acquisition can become overwhelming. It's not that the things we buy are inherently bad, but the belief that they define our happiness can lead us to pursue "more constantly." This is the pattern many of us get caught in—the chase for the next big thing, only to realize that when we get it, it doesn't fulfill us in the way we expected.

Letting go of these material attachments doesn't mean rejecting the world around us or living without any possessions. It simply means recognizing that our happiness is not dependent on what we own. It's about understanding that the things we accumulate can come and go, but our inner peace and contentment come from our mindset and how we choose to live.

PAIN

Life is temporary, and so are the challenges we face.

Just as we don't hold on too tightly to the good times, we must also learn not to let the bad times consume us. Life's constant ebb and flow of joy and sorrow is part of the human experience. We can cultivate a sense of inner peace by accepting that both happiness and suffering are transient. This understanding allows us to detach from the extremes, embracing the present moment without being overwhelmed. When we accept the temporary nature of all things, we find balance amidst life's ever-changing tides, freeing ourselves from the constant struggle of clinging or resisting.

SPIRITUAL ESSENCE

In the Bhagavad Gita, Lord Krishna frequently speaks about the temporary nature of the material world and its experiences. He emphasizes that everything in the physical world, including emotions, pleasure, pain, success, and failure, is transient. Krishna encourages individuals to recognize this impermanence and to cultivate a deeper connection with the eternal, unchanging soul (Atman) and the divine (Brahman). Below are a few key teachings that inspired me, where Krishna discusses the temporary nature of the world:

The impermanence of Life: In Chapter 2, Verse 14, Lord Krishna advises Arjuna to tolerate fleeting experiences of happiness and distress, emphasizing that these are temporary, like the changing seasons.

Eternal Soul: In Chapter 2, Verse 20, Krishna explains that while the physical body is temporary and perishable, the soul is eternal and unaffected by death.

Detachment from Material World: In Chapter 9, Verse 33, Krishna encourages detachment from the material world, suggesting that true peace is found through surrendering to the divine and focusing on the eternal.

Krishna teaches that by understanding the temporary nature of life and focusing on spiritual practices, one can transcend material attachments and find fulfillment through devotion to God.

Chapter 9

Healing is a process

Life isn't about constant validation from others—it's about cutting distractions and focusing on your growth. For many years, I shut my senses to people's judgments, focusing instead on what truly mattered: healing and rebuilding myself.

When I was going through a major heartbreak, I saw how quick people were to question and judge. These were often individuals with no understanding of my journey and no insight into the pain I carried. After all, why should I give weight to the opinions of those who have never walked a mile in my shoes?

People judged me for losing weight, never realizing the emotional toll of letting go of a decade-long relationship—the only relationship I had ever been in, one I fought for tirelessly.

But hope has its limits. The relationship I had clung to with every fiber of my being became a source of profound trauma. It was a bond that held me against my will, denying me the love, respect, and care I deserved.

It drained me emotionally, mentally, and physically, yet I stayed. I stayed because I loved him. I stayed because he wouldn't let go.

When I finally chose to leave, it wasn't because I stopped loving him—it was because I wanted to stay alive. After exhausting countless efforts to mend the relationship, I realized that leaving was not just a choice but the only path left to preserve my own well-being. My partner's unhealed pain had consumed me, and my savior complex had blinded me to the reality of our situation. I wore my invisible cape, determined to save him, only to fall and be broken in the process.

I felt deeply guilty for putting myself and my family in this situation—an irreversible burden I couldn't ignore. Adding to this were the challenges of living as an immigrant, far from the family I loved so deeply. I carried the weight of a quarter-million family loan, all while trying to navigate life in a foreign land. And then, there were the onlookers—people with no understanding of my reality—offering unsolicited judgments and advice. They wanted me to move on, as though healing were as simple as flipping a switch.

I am deeply thankful for the people who genuinely wished for my happiness and growth. However, there were others for whom my journey became nothing more than a topic of discussion, driven by curiosity rather than care. While some admired my resilience and the calm, centered demeanor I maintained through the storm, others viewed it with envy. Yet, what I endured internally was far more profound than I ever revealed.

Through it all, my family remained my unwavering support, giving me the space and time to heal and rebuild myself at my own pace.

I consciously distanced myself from social media, unsettling news, and movies that disrupted my peace of mind. That's when people assumed I had ghosted them. During this phase, I realized how difficult it was to find like-minded individuals in a world filled with noise and superficiality. With so many ongoing challenges, I felt too drained to invest energy in testing and building new friendships. It became easier to maintain surface-level interactions rather than risk the vulnerability of trust. This wasn't about losing faith in connections but about preserving my energy for the right ones.

Those days of solitude—when I stayed home instead of attending parties when I chose introspection over superficial distractions— were not losses. Every moment I spent working on myself made me stronger. I am grateful for those difficult moments, not because they were easy, but because they taught me to cut through the noise and distractions of life. They taught me to focus inward and rebuild my best version.

I didn't have the luxury of escaping my pain, but I developed the strength to confront it head-on.

I couldn't care less about the gossip that reaches me. I have never been concerned with who talks behind my back because I believe that what people say about others is often a reflection of their own insecurities or a desperate attempt to seek attention. A few rumors may still find their way to me, but I have far more meaningful things to focus on than entertaining baseless chatter.

Haters create gossip. Those who don't believe it ignore it. And those who do? They were never close enough to know me or my story in the first place. I see no reason to waste my energy clearing up false narratives—some things simply don't deserve a response. I trust that time has a way of unveiling the truth. If someone chooses to believe something without ever asking me, that says more about them than it does about me.

Just as I don't entertain gossip about myself, I don't spread it about others. If asked directly, I won't lie—but I also won't go out of my way to bring someone else down. I believe life has its own way of unmasking people, and in the end, the truth always finds its way.

Healing isn't linear, and growth isn't instantaneous, but every step I've taken on this journey has been worth it.

The Stages of Healing

1. **Anger**: This stage hit me hard, as I was filled with resentment over the injustice I faced. But I soon realized that holding onto anger was like drinking poison, hoping it would hurt someone else.

2. **Grief**: I mourned not only the relationship but also the dreams I had built around it. Grieving was painful, but it was necessary to let go.

3. **Guilt**: I carried guilt for a long time—for staying too long, for leaving, for everything in between.

4. **Blaming Others**: There were moments when I blamed my partner and even the circumstances for my pain. While it was natural to point fingers initially, I eventually saw that blaming others only prolonged my suffering and distracted me from my healing.

5. **Blaming Oneself**: I often thought, "What if I had done something differently?" or "Was it all my fault?" This self-blame weighed heavily on me.

6. **Acceptance**: Acceptance for me was a turning point, a quiet yet profound realization. It wasn't about denying the love I felt or pretending the pain didn't exist—it was about understanding that love shouldn't mean losing myself. I had to accept that I couldn't carry everything on my shoulders, not even for someone I once loved deeply. My time on this earth is limited, and I owe it to myself to live fully without being bound by hurtful compromises. Yes, it still hurts, and maybe it always will in some ways, but I've come to terms with that. Acceptance doesn't erase the scars; it gives me the strength to wear them proudly and move forward, knowing they're a part of me but not my whole story.

I began to see acceptance unfold in three dimensions—emotionally, practically, and spiritually. Practically, I learned that the definition of love differs from person to person. Emotionally, I accepted that each individual has their own capacity for emotional availability. Spiritually, I embraced the understanding that life simply happens, and always for a reason.

Right, healing is crucial because it ensures that you don't rely on others to fix what's broken within you. When you're healing properly, you don't use people as a distraction or a band-aid for your pain, nor do you unconsciously bleed your emotional wounds onto others. True healing allows you to stand firm on your own, embrace your pain, and work through it without imposing it on those around you. It's a process of becoming whole again so you can form healthy connections, nurture them, and not be driven by unresolved emotional needs.

While I might not be the only one who has encountered this pain, I am the only one living my life, walking my unique path. I refuse to let anyone discount the pain I've endured, just as I wouldn't diminish the struggles of another. Pain is deeply personal, and no one truly knows the weight someone carries. That's why I believe in empathy—our shared humanity demands it. If we can't help one another, the least we can do is refrain from judgment and focus on bettering ourselves instead. Compassion costs nothing, but its impact can be immeasurable.

Conclusion

Finding Clarity Through Reflection

When I first started writing this book, I carried mixed emotions—some unresolved, some bittersweet, and some I had long buried. As I put my thoughts into words, I realized that this wasn't just about telling my story but about understanding it & seeing my choices with newfound clarity.

With each chapter, I was not just narrating events—I was making peace with them. Life doesn't always give us instant answers, and sometimes, what feels like chaos is just a lesson in disguise. Looking back, I see now that every experience, every challenge, and every moment of doubt had its purpose. While I don't claim to have all the answers, I know one thing for certain—self-awareness and reflection bring a kind of wisdom that no external validation ever can.

This book is not just my story. It is an invitation for you, the reader, to reflect on your own journey, to find meaning in your own struggles, and to recognize that no path is without purpose.

If my experiences resonate with even one person, if they spark even a tiny moment of introspection, then sharing my journey has been worth it.

I may have started this book with a heavy heart, but I end it with a sense of peace. Not because everything is perfect, but because I now understand that everything happened exactly as it was meant to.

About the Author

 Hasti Leo is a lifelong learner with a deep passion for technology, education, and personal growth. With a career in IT, she enjoys creating solutions that improve business processes and drive efficiency. Alongside her work in technology, she has contributed to academia as a Teaching Assistant and Research Assistant, supporting students while continuing her own journey as a Ph.D. student.

Beyond her professional life, Hasti is a certified Yoga and Acupuncture practitioner, believing in the power of holistic healing to bring balance and well-being. She finds joy in volunteering with different organizations, offering her time to support and uplift others.

At her core, she is a spiritual seeker, always exploring life's deeper lessons. Through her experiences, she hopes to inspire others to embrace self-awareness, resilience, and continuous learning, believing that growth is a lifelong journey rather than a destination.

References

Chapter 1:

Demystifying the Eightfold Path: An Overview. https://buddhawisdom.app/demystifying-the-eightfold-path-an-overview/

What can the ancient Indian text Bhagavad Gita teach us about not putting too much of our identity and emotions into work | Clemson News. https://news.clemson.edu/what-the-ancient-indian-text-bhagavad-gita-can-teach-about-not-putting-too-much-of-our-identity-and-emotions-into-work/

The concept of the Four Self-Awareness Archetypes is inspired by interpretations of Jungian archetypes, emotional intelligence research, and mindfulness practices and is synthesized for this book.

Chapter 3:

*Dhammapada, translated by scholars such as **Thanissaro Bhikkhu** and **Eknath Easwaran**. The Dhammapada is one of the most revered texts in Theravada Buddhism.*

Chapter 7:

Ecclesiastes 3:1-8 - New International Version (NIV) "There is a time for everything and a season for every activity under the heavens..."

Psalm 27:14 - New International Version (NIV) "Wait for the Lord; be strong and take heart and wait for the Lord."

Romans 8:28 - New International Version (NIV) "And we know that in all things God works for the good of those who love him, who have been called according to his purpose."

Bhagavad Gita The Song of God https://www.holy-bhagavad-gita.org/chapter/2/verse/47

Chapter 8:

Bhagavad Gita, Translated by Eknath Easwaran, Swami Vivekananda, A.C. Bhaktivedanta Swami Prabhupada. These translations and commentaries explore the same themes of detachment, impermanence, and the soul's eternal nature.